XAMonline, Inc.
25 First Street, Suite 106
Cambridge, MA 02141
Toll Free: 1-800-509-4128
Email: info@xamonline.com
Web: www.xamonline.com
Fax: 1-617-583-5552

Library of Congress Cataloging-in-Publication Data

Wynne, Sharon A.
    MTEL Communications and Literacy Skills 01 Practice Test 2: Teacher Certification / Sharon A. Wynne. -1st ed.
    ISBN: 978-1-60787-208-5
    1. MTEL Communications and Literacy Skills 01 Practice Test 2
    2. Study Guides   3. MTEL   4. Teachers' Certification & Licensure
    5. Careers

Disclaimer:
The opinions expressed in this publication are the sole works of XAMonline and were created independently from the National Education Association, Educational Testing Service, or any State Department of Education, National Evaluation Systems or other testing affiliates.

Between the time of publication and printing, state specific standards as well as testing formats and website information may change that is not included in part or in whole within this product. Sample test questions are developed by XAMonline and reflect similar content as on real tests; however, they are not former tests. XAMonline assembles content that aligns with state standards but makes no claims nor guarantees teacher candidates a passing score. Numerical scores are determined by testing companies such as NES or ETS and then are compared with individual state standards. A passing score varies from state to state.

Printed in the United States of America   œ-1
MTEL Communications and Literacy Skills 01 Practice Test 2
ISBN: 978-1-60787-208-5

COMMUNICATION AND LITERACY SKILLS POST TEST

Reading Post Test

DIRECTIONS: *Read the following passages and answer the questions that follow.*

In elementary school we learned how to sort or _classify_ things. Early on, items were sorted by size, shape and color. As we grew up, matured, and were able to make larger connections and stretch our classifying skills to span a broader spectrum, we learned to look further at the details that separate or categorize things. Biologists often categorize or classify groups of animals by whether they are homologous or analogous. Homologous traits and analogous traits are quite different. Homologous traits are commonalities between subjects because they descend from the same place. For example, dogs, wolves, coyotes and the like have similar traits because they all come from the same ancestors. These animals all have similar body structure, bone structure, and jaw structure. Analogous traits are commonalities that are shared because of similar environmental influences. For example, polar bears and whales both have very thick skins to protect them from the cold Antarctic climate and they are adorable animals. But they do not share a common ancestor.

1. **What does the word "*classify*" mean in the passage?**

   A. classic
   B. identify
   C. justify
   D. Group

2. **What is the main idea of the passage?**

   A. Everything we need to know we learned in elementary school.
   B. One job of a biologist is to categorize animals.
   C. Groups can be categorized by whether they share homologous or analogous traits.
   D. All living things are connected in some way.

3. **From this passage the reader can conclude that**

   A. The author has an understanding of biology.
   B. The author used to be a biologist.
   C. The author has an interest in wild animals.
   D. The author used to teach elementary school.

4. **Why did the author include a common description of dogs, wolves, and coyotes?**

   A. To support the idea that the author knows something about dogs.
   B. To add context to the definition of homologous.
   C. To add context to the definition of analogous.
   D. To add validity to the author's claim that biologist have a need to classify animals.

5. **Animals are considered analogous because**

   A. They have all had to adapt to various external conditions.
   B. They all descend from the same ancestors.
   C. They all look alike and share a common physical feature.
   D. They live in the same part of the world.

6. **Which is an opinion presented in this passage?**

   A. As we grow and mature we, as humans, are able to extend our connections to make broader decisions.
   B. Biologists often categorize or classify animals by whether they are homologous or analogous.
   C. Dogs, wolves, and coyotes have similar traits.
   D. Polar bear and whales have adapted to the cold Arctic climate and are adorable.

7. **What type of organizational pattern did the author use in this passage?**

   A. Classification
   B. Compare-and-contrast
   C. Cause-and-effect
   D. Narrative

How important is the development of vocabulary within the confines of the classroom? It is very important between the ages of 1 and 17. This is when the greatest spurt of language learning takes place. Coincidentally, a bulk of this time period is when children spend the most time in school. However, _rote_ learning and constant work with dictionaries and reference materials are not the primary resources that will increase students' vocabularies. The largest portion of student vocabulary learning will occur while students are reading and conversing. When students are reading they must utilize their problem solving skills and use context clues to determine the meaning of unknown words. While students are conversing, they have the opportunity to learn from others whose vocabularies are broader than their own. The more experiences students have within the reading and conversing environments, the more extensive their vocabularies will become.

8. **What is another word that could be substituted for the word _rote_ in the passage?**

   A. classical
   B. monotonous
   C. repetitive
   D. remote

9. **What is the main idea of the passage?**

   A. The best way to expand student vocabularies is through authentic real-life experiences.
   B. Dictionaries and traditional reference materials have no place in today's classroom.
   C. Vocabulary should be taught sparingly in the classroom and be left to practical human experiences.
   D. Teachers need not work vocabulary into their everyday lessons because students will develop it naturally.

10. **What is the author's purpose in writing this piece?**

    A. To inform teachers that vocabulary is not best learned within the confines of the classroom.
    B. To teach students that they must surround themselves with smart people and good books.
    C. To persuade students to read more books and text less and interact in meaningful conversations.
    D. To inform those who interact with students that vocabulary is developed through a combination of classroom book work and real life learning.

11. **Who is the intended audience for this passage?**

    A. Parents of high school students.
    B. Anyone interested in how we learn.
    C. School administrators.
    D. Anyone between the ages of 1 and 17.

12. **What conclusion can be drawn from this passage?**

    A. The best learning will take place when the learner is actively involved in authentic, real-life experiences.
    B. The SAT should no longer have a vocabulary section included.
    C. Teachers should no longer use dictionaries and other reference materials in their classrooms.
    D. Students should be able to freely explore vocabulary development on their own through reading and conversation.

13. **What would be the best graphic representation to accompany this passage?**

    A. A pictograph that shows the number of books a high school freshman reads on average.
    B. A line graph that shows the number of ten letter words in a middle school student's vocabulary.
    C. A table that shows high frequency words that the average third grader should know.
    D. A bar graph that shows the average number of words in a person's vocabulary at various ages of life.

Perhaps it was Georgia O'Keefe's farming background that led her to paint the types of pictures that she did. Some of her better known pieces, "Black Iris" and "Red Poppy" are of oversized flowers. O'Keefe was born on November 15, 1887 in Sun Prairie, Wisconsin and lived on a farm until she was 16. At this time, her family moved to Williamsburg, Virginia.

After attending many different colleges around the country and enrolling in and teaching art classes and experimenting with her own style, she had her first solo art exhibition in 1917. The pieces exhibited were done in charcoals, oils, and watercolors. O'Keefe continued to paint landscapes and nature and even painted the bones that she found in the desert during some of her travels. Her paintings contain bold swirling colors that _border_ on abstract. Although some her paintings have a Southwestern flair to them, O'Keefe always considered herself an American artist, even after she had moved, and lived, in New Mexico.

14. **What does the word border mean in the second paragraph?**

   A. almost
   B. next to
   C. surround
   D. comparative

15. **What is the implied main idea of this passage?**

   A. Georgia O'Keefe came from a family of farmers and it is fascinating that she became an artist.
   B. Georgia O'Keefe's background in farming contributed to the genre of paintings she became famous for.
   C. Georgia O'Keefe considered herself an American artist when really she was a Southwestern artist.
   D. Georgia O'Keefe's paintings are well-known and original.

16. **Which group of people would MOST LIKELY be interested in reading this passage?**

   A. Residents of New Mexico.
   B. History teachers
   C. Art enthusiasts
   D. Landscape architects

17. **What happened after O'Keefe experimented with different mediums and styles of art?**

   A. She moved to New Mexico.
   B. She decided on creating abstract paintings.
   C. She had her first exhibition that featured only her paintings.
   D. She moved to Williamsburg, Virginia with her family.

18. **What argument does the author offer to support the idea that O'Keefe's farming background contributed to her artwork?**

   A. She used charcoals, oils and watercolors to create her masterpieces.
   B. O'Keefe's paintings contained bold swirling colors like the landscape of New Mexico.
   C. O'Keefe painted bold flowers, landscapes, and even bones found in the desert.
   D. Her paintings can be categorized as Southwestern in nature.

19. **Which would be the best diagram to accompany this passage?**

   A. A pie chart
   B. A bar graph
   C. A pictograph
   D. A timeline

It is not unheard of to hear someone comment about whether or not they are better at math or English. I have always been a better English student than math – math is confusing. This should not be the case however because math is a very _concrete_ subject whereas English is a more abstract, thought provoking, subject. English requires its students to rely on their own knowledge of topics and ideas to arrive at conclusions and make decision. Math, on the other hand, has rules and sequences. One topic in particular that often throws people a curve ball is fractions.

A fraction is a number that represents a part of a whole. The top number is called the _numerator_ and the bottom number is called the _denominator._ The denominator indicates the number of parts that make up the whole. A numerator is the number of parts that are being worked with. An example of a fraction is $\frac{2}{3}$. The number of parts that make up the whole is 3, and the number of parts that are being worked with is 2.

There are two types of fractions – a _proper fraction_ and an _improper fraction._ A proper fraction is a fraction whose numerator is less than the denominator – it is less than 1. An example of a proper fraction is $\frac{2}{3}$. An improper fraction is a fraction whose numerator is larger than the denominator – it is greater than 1. An example of an improper fraction is $\frac{10}{4}$.

20. **What does the author use the word _concrete_ in the passage to mean?**

    A. complicated
    B. logical
    C. solid
    D. open to interpretation

21. **Which detail supports the idea English is abstract?**

    A. It is thought provoking.
    B. The author is a better English student than math student.
    C. English requires the use of one's own knowledge and experiences.
    D. Fractions are a logical math topic.

22. **Why did the author use the words _on the other hand_ in the following sentence from the passage?**

    "Math, _on the other hand,_ has rules and sequences."

    A. To show that math is logical.
    B. To compare math and English as opposites.
    C. To show that fractions are like a topic in English.
    D. To demonstrate that math is better than English.

23. Why does the author say, "One topic in particular that often throws people a curve ball is fractions."

   A. Because fractions are useful in baseball.
   B. A baseball player must know fractions in order to throw a curve ball.
   C. A batter is often fooled by a curve ball because it is tricky.
   D. Fractions are very easy to understand just like a curve ball in baseball.

24. Does the author show any evidence of bias in this passage?

   A. Yes
   B. No

25. What is the BEST summary for the above passage?

   A. Fractions are made up of numerators and denominators.
   B. People often say they are better at math or English, but one topic that often gives people difficulty is fractions.
   C. In order to understand fractions, English students must know the difference between proper and improper fractions.
   D. A fraction is a number that represents a part of a whole and is an important topic for all to understand.

Alligators and crocodiles are not the same animal. Although both can be found in the Florida Everglades and even look alike, upon closer examination there are actually quite a few differences that _distinguish_ them from one another. A crocodile has a long narrow skull and has long jaws. Its teeth are always visible and overlap the upper jaw. An alligator has a bigger wider head and has a shorter jaw. Its teeth are only visible when its mouth is open. Despite their physical differences one overwhelming similarity between crocodiles and alligators is the fact that they are very intimidating. I for one would not want to get close enough to either of them to determine whether I can see their teeth when their mouth is closed.

26. **What does the word _distinguish_ mean in the passage?**

    A. To put out.
    B. To set apart.
    C. Are similar.
    D. To overlap.

27. **How does the author support the idea that crocodiles and alligators are different?**

    A. Alligators and crocodiles are not the same animal.
    B. They both can be found in the Florida Everglades.
    C. A crocodile's teeth are visible when its mouth is closed; an alligator's are not.
    D. Alligators are more intimidating than crocodiles.

28. **Who would MOST LIKELY be the most interested in reading this article?**

    A. A resident of the Florida Everglades.
    B. A zoologist that is in charge of the alligator exhibit.
    C. A copywriter for National Geographic Magazine.
    D. A student doing a report on crocodiles.

29. **What conclusion can be drawn about the author?**

    A. The author finds it fascinating that alligators and crocodiles can be identified by their jaws.
    B. The author does not like reptiles – especially alligators and crocodiles.
    C. The author would only like to observe alligators or crocodiles at the zoo in a controlled environment.
    D. The author prefers crocodiles over alligators.

30. **The author states that it is a fact that alligators and crocodiles are intimidating. Is this a true statement?**

    A. Yes – it is a fact.
    B. No – it is an opinion.

| Year | Unprovoked Bites[1] | | | | Provoked[2] Bites | Total Bites |
	Major[3]	Fatal	Minor[4]	Total	Total	Total
2005	6	(1)	1	7	2	9
2004	9	(2)	3	12	1	13
2003	9	(1)	1	10	2	12
2002	7	(0)	4	11	4	15
2001	11	(3)	5	16	9	25
2000	7	(0)	3	10	13	23
1999	5	(0)	5	10	6	16
1998	3	(0)	2	5	4	9
1997	3	(1)	1	4	4	8
1996	4	(0)	1	5	8	13
1995	9	(0)	4	13	9	22
1994	5	(0)	6	11	9	20
1993	8	(2)	5	13	6	19
1992	5	(0)	1	6	9	15
1991	5	(0)	5	10	10	20
1990	3	(0)	10	13	4	17
1989	4	(0)	6	10	3	13
1988	6	(1)	3	9	9	18
1987	3	(1)	6	9	4	13
1986	3	(0)	10	13	10	23
1985	4	(1)	2	6	1	7
1984	5	(1)	0	5	4	9
1983	5	(0)	1	6	3	9
1982	4	(0)	3	7	0	7
1981	5	(0)	3	8	2	10
1980	4	(0)	0	4	1	5
1979	2	(0)	0	2	0	2
1978	6	(1)	0	6	1	7
1977	13	(1)	1	14	0	14
1976	2	(0)	0	2	0	2
1975	4	(0)	0	4	1	5
1974	4	(0)	0	4	0	4
1973	3	(1)	0	3	0	3
1972	3	(0)	0	3	1	4
1971	3	(0)	0	3	0	3

Taken from: Florida Fish and Wildlife Conservation Commission Historic Alligator Bites on Humans in Florida; Last Updated 10/23/2005

31. When did the most provoked alligator bites occur?

A. 2001
B. 2000
C. 1986
D. 1977

The last known case of smallpox in the United States occurred in Texas in 1949. Eight cases were reported and 1 death occurred. Smallpox has all but become extinct in the United States thanks to an English doctor named Edward Jenner. In 1796 Jenner made a stunning discovery that dairymaids who had contracted cowpox, a less serious disease than smallpox, never developed the smallpox disease even when they were exposed to it. To further solidify his discovery, Jenner infected an 8-year-old boy with cowpox and exposed the boy to smallpox 6 weeks later. Consequently, the boy did not develop any smallpox symptoms. Jenner then coined this process vaccine because the word "vaca" is a root which means "cow" in Latin.

There have been no further smallpox vaccinations given since 1972 in the United States with the exception of military personnel. Vaccines to this segment of the population ceased in 1990 and the world is still free of smallpox.

32. **What MOST LIKELY resulted from this first vaccine?**

A. Other vaccinations were invented to prevent other communicable diseases.
B. Edward Jennar won a distinguished medical research award.
C. Many people died from cowpox and smallpox unnecessarily.
D. Military personnel brought the disease back with them to the United States from foreign countries.

33. **Which statement would the author most likely agree with?**

A. Military personnel deserve our admiration and utmost respect.
B. Children should not be used to test new vaccinations.
C. Vaccinations are an important piece in keeping the United States healthy and disease free.
D. Only people in Texas should have received the first vaccinations.

Recommended Immunization Schedule
for Ages 0-6 Years

UNITED STATES • 2007

Range of recommended ages   Catch-up Immunization   Certain high-risk groups

Vaccine ▼ Age ▶	Birth	1 month	2 months	4 months	6 months	12 months	15 months	18 months	19-23 months	2-3 years	4-6 years
Hepatitis B[1]	HepB	HepB		see footnote 1		HepB				HepB Series	
Rotavirus			Rota	Rota	Rota						
Diphtheria, Tetanus, Pertussis			DTaP	DTaP	DTaP		DTaP				DTaP
Haemophilus Influenzae type b			Hib	Hib	Hib	Hib			Hib		
Pneumococcal[2]			PCV	PCV	PCV	PCV					
Inactivated Poliovirus			IPV	IPV		IPV					IPV
Influenza[3]						Influenza (Yearly)					
Measles, Mumps, Rubella						MMR					MMR
Varicella						Varicella					Varicella
Hepatitis A						HepA (2 doses)					
Meningococcal											

---

34. What conclusion can be drawn from the chart above?

A. Only those children in a high-risk group receive the Hepatitis A vaccine.
B. Children receive most of their vaccinations between the ages of 6 and 18 months of age.
C. Children receive most of their vaccinations at birth.
D. If a child misses a vaccination at a certain age, they are unable to receive it later.

35. What is the main idea of the passage?

A. Dairymaids were unable to contract the smallpox disease because their occupation made them immune.
B. Edward Jenner was a veterinarian that stumbled upon the vaccination for smallpox.
C. Smallpox could have been a destructive epidemic that was avoided thanks to the discovery of Dr. Edward Jenner.
D. It is important for military personnel to get vaccinated before returning to the United States.

36. **What can be concluded from the statement, "There have been no further smallpox vaccinations given since 1972 in the United States…"**

A. Smallpox only existed in foreign countries.
B. Smallpox was no longer a threat to the United States and people no longer needed to get vaccinated.
C. Smallpox will make a comeback within the next few decades.
D. It took a long time for people to accept that Jenner's vaccinations were needed and successful.

Recently developed within the past several years, Pilates is an exercise system that evolved from its creator Joseph Pilates as a way to strengthen both the mind and the body together. Many people have gravitated to Pilates as a way to achieve a healthy, toned appearance without looking too "bulky". In addition, Pilates increases good posture, improves flexibility and *agility*.

Pilates is very different than weight training in that it elongates the muscles while strengthening them. This is what eliminates the "bulky" look achieved by lifting weights. Building the core is a focus in Pilates. The core refers to the center of the body or the abdomen. People are drawn to Pilates because it helps to tone and flatten the hard to tame abdominal area.

Safety is another benefit that Pilates boasts. If the muscles of the body are trained in a fluid, smooth motion and technique, the muscles will work more efficiently and posture will be improved and injuries will be prevented.

37. **Why might people be interested in Pilates?**

A. They want to get bulkier looking muscles.
B. They want to increase their cardiovascular endurance.
C. They want to tone their muscles and improve their posture.
D. They want to have Joseph Pilates personally train them.

38. When the author says that, "Pilates increases good posture, improves flexibility and agility," that is a(n)

A. Fact
B. Opinion

39. From the passage, it can be assumed that

A. Only celebrities and those with a lot of money can do Pilates training.
B. Pilates training would be a beneficial mode of exercise for all ages.
C. Dancers will greatly benefit from doing Pilates daily.
D. Joseph Pilates only developed this form of exercise because he did not enjoy running.

40. Which is the best synonym for the word <u>agility</u>?

A. relationships
B. power
C. endurance
D. self-confidence

41. What is another way the information in the passage could be delivered?

A. A poster.
B. An infomercial.
C. A Venn Diagram
D. A before and after diagram

42. What two components is Pilates aimed at improving?

A. The mind and the body together.
B. The muscles and the core.
C. The abdominal area and the mind.
D. The legs and the core.

Writing Post Test

1 Nursing is a great career for women whom have or want to have young children someday. **2** They can works very flexible schedules either part time or full time. **3** healthcare is an ever expanding feild so jobs are predicted to be plentiful in many years to come. **4** There are many different areas where people can match their interests to a particular nursing specialty. **5** For example, if one is interested in children the elderly, or feet even there is a place for everyone. **6** Even though there are a lot of positive reasons for women to choose nursing as a career, the negatives must also be considered before embarking on a lifelong career choice. **7** However there will be negative aspects to any job.

1. **What would be the best way to combine sentences 1 and 2 to make a complete topic sentence?**

   A. Nursing is a great career for women who have, or want to have children someday, because the schedules are flexible and offer a lot of full and part time opportunities.
   B. Nursing is a great career for women who have, or want to have children on the other hand it offers flexible full and part time schedules.
   C. Nursing is a great career for women who currently have, or want to have, a family due to the full and part time flexible scheduling.
   D. Nursing is a great career for women who currently have, or want to have, a family furthermore because of the full time and part time scheduling.

2. **Which of these ideas does not help to develop the main idea of the passage?**

   A. Healthcare is an ever expanding field.
   B. People can match their interests to a particular field in nursing.
   C. Even people interested in feet can become a nurse.
   D. There are negative aspects to any job.

3. **Which part of the passage should be corrected to use the correct relative pronoun?**

   A. Part 1: Change "whom" to "who"
   B. Part 3: Change "so" to "that"
   C. Part 4: Change "where" to "which"
   D. Part 6: Change "on" to "in"

4. **Which verb needs to be changed to make the sentence correct?**

   A. Part 1: have
   B. Part 2: works
   C. Part 3: be
   D. Part 4: are

5. **Which word is misspelled?**

   A. Part 1: someday
   B. Part 2: flexible
   C. Part 3: feild
   D. Part 6: though

6. **How should sentence 5 be rewritten?**

   A. For example, if one is interested in children – the elderly – or feet – even there is a place for everyone.
   B. For example if one is interested in children, the elderly feet, or even there is a place for everyone.
   C. For example, if one is interested in children, the elderly, or feet even, there is a place for everyone.
   D. For example: if one is interested in children – the elderly; or feet even, there is a place for everyone.

7. **What needs to be capitalized in the passage?**

   A. Part 1: Women
   B. Part 3: Healthcare
   C. Part 5: Elderly
   D. Part 6: Nursing

1 The school staff at Lincoln Middle School was not prepared for the increase in the number of students whom would be entering the 6th grade in the upcoming school year. **2** Several changes needed to be made in order to accommodate the largely intended increase in the student body. **3** First another classroom needed to be found. **4** This would be a daunting task but there were several possibilities to consider. **5** Moving the computer lab was one option. **6** More computers could be added to the library and the other four labs that were spred around the building. **7** Lincoln middle would be short a computer lab, but would have gained another classroom. **8** Next, a new staff member would have to be hired to work inside the new classroom. **9** This too would not be a problem because there was an over abundance of applicants that had applied for teaching positions that year. **10** The biggest problem would be the amount of teaching resources available. **11** More textbooks and workbooks would need to be ordered. **12** It was questionable if the teachers resources would all arrive in time for the new school year to begin.

8. **If a new paragraph was to be started at line 3, what would be the best transitional phrase to use?**

   A. Last but not least,
   B. In the meantime,
   C. First and foremost,
   D. The first thing at hand,

9. **Which part of the passage should be revised to correct an error in the use of prepositions?**

   A. Part 1: Change "at" to "in"
   B. Part 2: Change "in" to "of"
   C. Part 8: Change "inside" to "in"
   D. Part 12: Change "in" to "on"

10. **Which word is misspelled?**

    A. Part 1: increase
    B. Part 5: four
    C. Part 5: spred
    D. Part 10: biggest

11. **Which word needs a change in capitalization?**

    A. Part 1: Lincoln
    B. Part 1: grade
    C. Part 7: Middle
    D. Part 12: school year

12. **Which part of the passage requires a comma?**

    A. Part 1: The school staff at Lincoln Middle School, was not prepared for the increase in the number of students whom would be entering the 6th grade in the upcoming school year.

    B. Part 3: First, another classroom needed to be found.

    C. Part 6: More computers could be added to the library, and the other four labs that were spread around the building.

    D. Part 9: This too, would not be a problem because there was an over abundance of applicants that had applied for teaching positions that year.

13. **Which part of the passage requires an apostrophe?**

    A. Part 1: students
    B. Part 4: possibilities
    C. Part 6: computers
    D. Part 12: teachers

1 Their are many things living objects need in order to survive. **2** All living things need food, water, and air. **3** Plants get their food from the rich nutrients in soil, water from rain and they pull air in through their leaves. **4** Animals get food by hunting pray, they too get water from rain, but find sources where it has collected, and they get their air from the oxygen that plants and trees emit. **5** Humans are like animals. **6** We need food water, and air to survive. **7** We have an overabundance of food and water supplies and feel that we cannot live without food. **8** However, we can live without food for several weeks if necessary. **9** We can survive without water for only a few days. **10** However we can only live without air for as little as 3 to 6 minutes. **11** Air is essential for humans hearts and brains to function properly.

14. **If another paragraph were to be added, what would be the best topic sentence?**

    A. Humans think that food and water are the most important things needed for their survival.
    B. When humans breathe air into their lungs it serves several different purposes.
    C. Humans and animals are alike because both require oxygen for their survival.
    D. When humans consume food, it goes through several processes in order to be turned into fuel for the human body.

15. **Which sentence could be deleted from the passage because of redundancy?**

    A. Sentence 7
    B. Sentence 8
    C. Sentence 9
    D. Sentence 10

16. **Which sentence should have a period instead of a comma?**

    A. Sentence 2
    B. Sentence 4
    C. Sentence 6
    D. Sentence 7

17. **What is the correct way to revise sentence 6?**

    A. We, need food, water, and air to survive.
    B. We need food, water and air to survive.
    C. We need food water and air to survive.
    D. We need food, water, and air to survive.

18. **How should sentence 7 be revised to be clearer?**

    A. In the United States, there is an overabundance of food and water.
    B. Supplies of food and water are in overabundance within the United States for humans.
    C. Food and water supplies in abundance are available in a plentiful manner in the United States.
    D. An overabundance of food and water and air is available for citizens of the United States.

19. Which sentence contains the wrong form of their/there/they're?

   A. Sentence 1
   B. Sentence 3
   C. Sentence 4
   D. Sentence 11

20. Which sentence has a misspelled word in it?

   A. Sentence 4
   B. Sentence 5
   C. Sentence 6
   D. Sentence 7

21. Which sentence is missing a comma?

   A. Sentence 1
   B. Sentence 3
   C. Sentence 5
   D. Sentence 10

22. Which sentence needs an apostrophe added?

   A. Sentence 3
   B. Sentence 4
   C. Sentence 5
   D. Sentence 11

1 Earthquakes are sometimes something to fear. **2** With the invention of the seismograph however, they have become more predictable. **3** Scientists has predicted the potential for earthquakes with a reasonable degree of accuracy. **4** Sometimes even scientists have predicted an earthquake but it has never occurred. **5** Some believe that this is a good mistake. **6** It is better to have predicted an Earthquake incorrectly than not predict it at all.

23. **What is the topic sentence of the passage?**

    A. Sentence 1
    B. Sentence 2
    C. Sentence 3
    D. Sentence 4

24. **Which sentence shows some redundancy?**

    A. Sentence 3
    B. Sentence 4
    C. Sentence 9
    D. Sentence 11

25. **If another paragraph were to be added to this passage, what is the best topic sentence?**

    A. One earthquake that scientists were able to predict by using a seismograph was X.
    B. The definition of an earthquake is...
    C. The biggest earthquake to hit the United States was...
    D. Earthquakes have been recorded the most in...

26. **Which sentence has a verb in its incorrect form?**

    A. Sentence 1
    B. Sentence 3
    C. Sentence 4
    D. Sentence 6

27. **Which sentence has misplaced or dangling modifiers?**

    A. Sentence 1
    B. Sentence 2
    C. Sentence 3
    D. Sentence 4

28. **Which sentence contains an error in capitalization?**

    A. Sentence 4
    B. Sentence 5
    C. Sentence 6
    D. Sentence 7

29. **Which sentence is missing a comma?**

    A. Sentence 3
    B. Sentence 4
    C. Sentence 9
    D. Sentence 12

30. **Which topic would be the best focus for the introduction to come before the first sentence of this passage?**

    A. Inventions
    B. Famous scientists
    C. Things we are scared of
    D. Things that shake

1 Certain plants and animals have been able to adapt well to the extreme conditions of the desert. **2** Since there is very little water available in the desert plants and animals have had to evolve and change. **3** Some things that are unique to plants in the desert are their thick leaves. **4** The thick leaves are vats used for storing water. **5** One such plant that has adapted very successfully is the cactus. **6** But the cactus doesn't stop there! **7** It even protects its supply of water with its long pointy spines. **8** These spines keep predators from tapping into the cacti's thick, succulent leaves. **9** Water is stored in the leaves of the cactus.

31. **What is the thesis statement for this essay?**

    A. Sentence 1
    B. Sentence 2
    C. Sentence 3
    D. Sentence 4

32. **Which sentence does not contribute to the development of the main idea of the passage?**

    A. Sentence 5
    B. Sentence 6
    C. Sentence 7
    D. Sentence 1

33. **Which sentence should come first in the next paragraph if the essay were to be continued?**

    A. Not even a small hummingbird would try to penetrate the spines of a cactus.
    B. Many people have be pricked by the spines of a cactus.
    C. One animal that has adapted well to the extreme conditions of the desert is the Gila Monster.
    D. People are not able to live in the desert for long periods of time because of the lack of moisture.

34. **Which sentence could be deleted from the passage because it is repetitive?**

    A. Sentence 6
    B. Sentence 7
    C. Sentence 8
    D. Sentence 9

35. **What would be the best way to combine sentences 1 and 2 to create a new topic sentence?**

  A. Due to the extremely dry conditions in the desert, the plants and animals that survive there have had to adapt.
  B. The plants and animals that call the desert their home are able to do so because they have adapted to the extremely dry conditions there.
  C. No water means that plants and animals have had to adapt.
  D. The desert causes the things that live there to adapt to its conditions.

The following sentences contain two errors each (e.g., in construction, grammar, usage, spelling, capitalization, punctuation). Rewrite the text so that the errors are addressed and the original meaning is maintained.

36. **Mozart used an instrument called the harpsichord and the piano to create a lot of beautiful concertos which are still enjoy today.**

37. **A teacher must be savvy when grading research and term papers and have the ability to recognize plagiarizing student work.**

38. **After watching the two commercials back to back that was trying to sell the same product I came to the conclusion that the first commercial was more interesting than the second one.**

39. **Upon checking the applicants references the company found that the candidate was not as reliable as was initially believed to be.**

40. **The woman gathered together at the house of there friend Nancy to discuss the current political agenda.**

41. **The pie had a flaky crusts that made it deliciously and irresistible.**

42. **Less U.S. citizens are visiting European countries because of the dwindles in the current exchange rate.**

Essay #1: **Use the passage below to prepare a summary of 100-150 words.**

Curriculums within schools are the depth and breadth of the education the students will receive. They are living breathing documents which provide the foundation for the entire educational process in this country. Curriculums are necessary evils to many developers; complex structures which grow, change, and never seem to be quite finished. In the ideal, the curriculum is what is taught to the students, the content. It is through this content that learners societal and subject matter needs are all addressed.

Historically, curriculums have not always been as influential as designers would like them for the students they serve. In recent times, more attention has been paid to the manner in which curriculum effects what is actually being taught in classrooms. Federal and State mandates have imposed this increase in attention. Governmental influence into education has steadily increased reaching its ebb in 2001 with the passage of the No Child Left Behind (NCLB) legislation.

While the legislation itself does not require a federally aligned or mandated curriculum, it does hold schools accountable for making progress. This accountability piece is within itself a demand for curriculum accountability. States have imposed a variety of mandates in order to meet these requirements some in the form of required assessments and standards which provide schools with a broad general focus upon which to build their curriculums.

Reaching its pinnacle for discussion in the 1990s, the standards-based reform movement provides schools with a basis upon which to build their own individual curriculums. As adopted this movement provides individual school entities the basic understanding of areas which need to be covered by the curriculum at specific target grade levels. These same areas are then assessed utilizing state level assessments, thus tracking progress and providing accountability in order to meet the requirements of the NCLB Act.

At this point, it becomes the responsibility of the school entity to transfer this broad standard level information into a meaningful curriculum which is then delivered to its students. The school system typically takes this broad information provided for key benchmark grade levels and breaks it into meaningful, developmentally appropriate chunks to cover all grade levels and subjects. Systems must also consider skills beyond those being assessed which are important aspects in order to provide a broader more appropriate curriculum, rather than a narrow, only what is assessed one.

Standards-based education has taken the understanding of schools and systems to a higher level in regards to the content. However, with the passage of NCLB many curriculums have unfortunately narrowed to a scope which is only inclusive of the areas being assessed at targeted grade levels. It will be throughout the next few years that systems will have to combine the ideas of standards-based educational reform with best practices in curriculum development to reach a compromise which meets the needs of all students within its system. The combination of both approaches will help to move students to higher levels of academic success, which can only serve to move the entire society to higher levels as well.

Essay #2: Read the passages that follow about drug testing in schools. Then follow the instructions for writing your composition.

Drug Testing in Schools Is Necessary to Eliminate the amount of Drug Addicts in Society

School systems have a responsibility to educate and protect their students. By employing the use of drug tests, schools can provide additional education opportunities to ensure students do not become addicts. Additionally, it sends the message to all members that drugs are wrong.

Drug Testing in Schools is Wrong

Schools are places for learning, not police action. Students in schools have the right to privacy and should not be considered guilty until proven innocent when the same standard is not applied to other portions of society. While drug use is a problem, it is not the responsibility of the school system to risk the dignity of all students based on a fear of what a few students may be engaged in during their off school time.

Your purpose is to write a composition that will be read by a classroom instructor, in which you will take a position on the issues described in the passages about drug testing in schools. Be sure to use logical arguments to defend your position and include appropriate examples.

ANSWER KEY

Reading

1. D
2. C
3. A
4. B
5. A
6. D
7. A
8. C
9. A
10. D
11. B
12. A
13. D
14. A
15. B
16. C
17. C
18. C
19. D
20. B
21. C
22. B
23. C
24. A
25. B
26. B
27. C
28. D

29. C
30. B
31. B
32. A
33. C
34. B
35. C
36. B
37. C
38. A
39. B
40. C
41. B
42. A

Writing

1. A
2. D
3. A
4. B
5. C
6. C
7. B
8. C
9. C
10. C
11. C
12. B

13. D
14. B
15. A
16. B
17. D
18. A
19. A
20. A
21. D
22. D
23. B
24. B
25. A
26. B
27. B
28. C
29. B
30. C
31. A
32. A
33. C
34. C
35. B
36. See rationale
37. See rationale
38. See rationale
39. See rationale
40. See rationale
41. See rationale
42. See rationale

Reading Post Test Rationales

DIRECTIONS: *Read the passages and answer the questions that follow.*

In elementary school we learned how to sort or *classify* things. Early on, items were sorted by size, shape and color. As we grew up, matured, and were able to make larger connections and stretch our classifying skills to span a broader spectrum, we learned to look further at the details that separate or categorize things. Biologists often categorize or classify groups of animals by whether they are homologous or analogous.

Homologous traits and analogous traits are quite different. Homologous traits are commonalities between subjects because they descend from the same place. For example, dogs, wolves, coyotes and the like have similar traits because they all come from the same ancestors. These animals all have similar body structure, bone structure, and jaw structure. Analogous traits are commonalities that are shared because of similar environmental influences. For example, polar bears and whales both have very thick skins to protect them from the cold Antarctic climate and they are adorable animals. But they do not share a common ancestor.

1. **What does the word "*classify*" mean in the passage?**

   A. classic
   B. identify
   C. justify
   D. Group

Answer D: The context clue "sort" gives the reader the idea that "group" means the same thing.

2. **What is the main idea of the passage?**

   A. Everything we need to know we learned in elementary school.
   B. One job of a biologist is to categorize animals.
   C. Groups can be categorized by whether they share homologous or analogous traits.
   D. All living things are connected in some way.

Answer C: Thesis statements generally sum up the main idea of a passage or essay and thesis statements are normally the last sentence of the first paragraph. The last sentence of the first paragraph says that, "Biologists often categorize or classify groups of animals by whether they are homologous or analogous."

3. **From this passage the reader can conclude that**

    A. The author has an understanding of biology.
    B. The author used to be a biologist.
    C. The author has an interest in wild animals.
    D. The author used to teach elementary school.

Answer A: The only logical answer here is A. There isn't any way to tell if the author used to be a biologist. The author might be interested in wild animals, but Choice A is still a better choice. There is nothing in the passage that leads us to believe that the author used to teach elementary school.

4. **Why did the author include a common description of dogs, wolves, and coyotes?**

    A. To support the idea that the author knows something about dogs.
    B. To add context to the definition of homologous.
    C. To add context to the definition of analogous.
    D. To add validity to the author's claim that biologists have a need to classify animals.

Answer B: When authors write, they must add support to their claims and add supporting details to help the author understand the information better. The author describes the canine family to support the definition of homologous and make it more understandable for the reader.

5. **Animals are considered analogous because**

    A. They have all had to adapt to various external conditions.
    B. They all descend from the same ancestors.
    C. They all look alike and share a common physical feature.
    D. They live in the same part of the world.

Answer A: This question asks the reader to examine the details and find the definition within the passage. Choice A is the definition analogous.

6. **Which is an opinion presented in this passage?**

   A. As we grow and mature we, as humans, are able to extend our connections to make broader decisions.
   B. Biologists often categorize or classify animals by whether they are homologous or analogous.
   C. Dogs, wolves, and coyotes have similar traits.
   D. Polar bear and whales have adapted to the cold Arctic climate and are adorable.

Answer D: An opinion is something that can be argues. The key word in Choice D that alerts the reader that it is in fact an opinion, is the word "adorable".

7. **What type of organizational pattern did the author use in this passage?**

   A. Classification
   B. Compare-and-contrast
   C. Cause-and-effect
   D. Narrative

Answer A: This passage defines homologous and analogous and offers details to support both definitions. Therefore, this is a classification passage.

How important is the development of vocabulary within the confines of the classroom? It is very important between the ages of 1 and 17. This is when the greatest spurt of language learning takes place. Coincidentally, a bulk of this time period is when children spend the most time in school. However, _rote_ learning and constant work with dictionaries and reference materials are not the primary resources that will increase students' vocabularies. The largest portion of student vocabulary learning will occur while students are reading and conversing. When students are reading they must utilize their problem solving skills and use context clues to determine the meaning of unknown words. While students are conversing, they have the opportunity to learn from others whose vocabularies are broader than their own. The more experiences students have within the reading and conversing environments, the more extensive their vocabularies will become.

8. What is another word that could be substituted for the word _rote_ in the passage?

    A. classical
    B. monotonous
    C. repetitive
    D. remote

Answer C: Rote learning is repetitive. Although on first glance, Choice B "monotonous" would seem to work, rote is more repetitive than it is monotonous.

9. What is the main idea of the passage?

    A. The best way to expand student vocabularies is through authentic real-life experiences.
    B. Dictionaries and traditional reference materials have no place in today's classroom.
    C. Vocabulary should be taught sparingly in the classroom and be left to practical human experiences.
    D. Teachers need not work vocabulary into their everyday lessons because students will develop it naturally.

Answer A: The main idea must cover the whole passage. In other words, it must sum up the whole passage in one sentence. Choice A is the only one that accomplishes this. The remaining choices are simply not true.

10. What is the author's purpose in writing this piece?

A. To inform teachers that vocabulary is not best learned within the confines of the classroom.
B. To teach students that they must surround themselves with smart people and good books.
C. To persuade students to read more books and text less and interact in meaningful conversations.
D. To inform those who interact with students that vocabulary is developed through a combination of classroom book work and real life learning.

Answer D: This passage was clearly written to inform. Therefore, the reader must decide if it was written to inform teachers or anyone that interact and have a vested interest in their vocabulary development. Looking at the broader picture, the passage is meant to inform anyone who has an interest in student's vocabulary development.

11. Who is the intended audience for this passage?

A. Parents of high school students.
B. Anyone interested in how we learn.
C. School administrators.
D. Anyone between the ages of 1 and 17.

Answer B: Similar to Question 10, it is necessary to look at the broader picture to answer this question. This passage is for anyone that is interested in how we as humans learn.

12. What conclusion can be drawn from this passage?

A. The best learning will take place when the learner is actively involved in authentic, real-life experiences.
B. The SAT should no longer have a vocabulary section included.
C. Teachers should no longer use dictionaries and other reference materials in their classrooms.
D. Students should be able to freely explore vocabulary development on their own through reading and conversation.

Answer A: Drawing conclusions requires us to combine our own knowledge with that offered in the passage by the author. We can decide from the information offered in this passage that the best learning, specifically vocabulary in this passage, is best accomplished through authentic, real-world experiences. Choice D may work, but without the guidance of teachers and educators, students may be heading down the wrong path.

13. **What would be the best graphic representation to accompany this passage?**

    A. A pictograph that shows the number of books a high school freshman reads on average.

    B. A line graph that shows the number of ten letter words in a middle school student's vocabulary.

    C. A table that shows high frequency words that the average third grader should know.

    D. A bar graph that shows the average number of words in a person's vocabulary at various ages of life.

Answer D: Although all of the graphics may relate to the passage, Choice D is the most connected. Choice C is too specific to third grade and leaves out a vast number of people. Choice D applies to many more people and therefore is the best choice.

Perhaps it was Georgia O'Keefe's farming background that led her to paint the types of pictures that she did. Some of her better known pieces, "Black Iris" and "Red Poppy" are of oversized flowers. O'Keefe was born on November 15, 1887 in Sun Prairie, Wisconsin and lived on a farm until she was 16. At this time, her family moved to Williamsburg, Virginia.

After attending many different colleges around the country and enrolling in and teaching art classes and experimenting with her own style, she had her first solo art exhibition in 1917. The pieces exhibited were done in charcoals, oils, and watercolors. O'Keefe continued to paint landscapes and nature and even painted the bones that she found in the desert during some of her travels. Her paintings contain bold swirling colors that _border_ on abstract. Although some her paintings have a Southwestern flair to them, O'Keefe always considered herself an American artist, even after she had moved, and lived, in New Mexico.

14. What does the word border mean in the second paragraph?

A. almost
B. next to
C. surround
D. comparative

Answer A: The passage is saying that O'Keefe's paintings are close to being coined abstract paintings. Therefore the best synonym for border is "almost".

15. What is the implied main idea of this passage?

A. Georgia O'Keefe came from a family of farmers and it is fascinating that she became an artist.
B. Georgia O'Keefe's background in farming contributed to the genre of paintings she became famous for.
C. Georgia O'Keefe considered herself an American artist when really she was a Southwestern artist.
D. Georgia O'Keefe's paintings are well-known and original.

Answer B: The main idea must be a sentence that tells about the whole passage and not just a small detail. Choice B is specific enough and describes the essence of the whole passage. Choice D may work, but it is too broad and not specific enough.

16. **Which group of people would MOST LIKELY be interested in reading this passage?**

   A. Residents of New Mexico.
   B. History teachers
   C. Art enthusiasts
   D. Landscape architects

Answer C: Although certain history teachers (Choice B) might be interested in this passage, most likely art enthusiasts would be most interested in learning about Georgia O'Keefe's background.

17. **What happened after O'Keefe experimented with different mediums and styles of art?**

   A. She moved to New Mexico.
   B. She decided on creating abstract paintings.
   C. She had her first exhibition that featured only her paintings.
   D. She moved to Williamsburg, Virginia with her family.

Answer C: This is a sequencing question. The reader must go back into the passage, find the section that talks about O'Keefe using charcoals, oils, and watercolors and read to find out what happens next. Choice C is the best answer.

18. **What argument does the author offer to support the idea that O'Keefe's farming background contributed to her artwork?**

   A. She used charcoals, oils and watercolors to create her masterpieces.
   B. O'Keefe's paintings contained bold swirling colors like the landscape of New Mexico.
   C. O'Keefe painted bold flowers, landscapes, and even bones found in the desert.
   D. Her paintings can be categorized as Southwestern in nature.

Answer C: It is necessary to make a connection between farming and O'Keefe's paintings. Choice C connects flowers, landscapes, and bones to nature. This is the connection to farming.

19. Which would be the best diagram to accompany this passage?

A. A pie chart
B. A bar graph
C. A pictograph
D. A timeline

Answer D: Especially when biographies or recounts of a person's life need to put into a visual representation, the best method is a timeline which will show the important milestones in a person's life and connect those milestones to dates.

It is not unheard of to hear someone comment about whether or not they are better at math or English. I have always been a better English student than math – math is confusing. This should not be the case however because math is a very _concrete_ subject whereas English is a more abstract, thought provoking, subject. English requires its students to rely on their own knowledge of topics and ideas to arrive at conclusions and make decision. Math, on the other hand, has rules and sequences. One topic in particular that often throws people a curve ball is fractions.

A fraction is a number that represents a part of a whole. The top number is called the _numerator_ and the bottom number is called the _denominator._ The denominator indicates the number of parts that make up the whole. A numerator is the number of parts that are being worked with. An example of a fraction is $\frac{2}{3}$. The number of parts that make up the whole is 3, and the number of parts that are being worked with is 2.

There are two types of fractions – a _proper fraction_ and an _improper fraction._ A proper fraction is a fraction whose numerator is less than the denominator – it is less than 1. An example of a proper fraction is $\frac{2}{3}$. An improper fraction is a fraction whose numerator is larger than the denominator – it is greater than 1. An example of an improper fraction is $\frac{10}{4}$.

20. What does the author use the word _concrete_ in the passage to mean?

    A. complicated
    B. logical
    C. solid
    D. open to interpretation

Answer B: "Concrete" is a word that has multiple meanings. In this passage, the best synonym is logical. The sentence compares math, a concrete subject, to English an abstract, subject. Therefore, Choice B is the best answer.

21. Which detail supports the idea English is abstract?

    A. It is thought provoking.
    B. The author is a better English student than math student.
    C. English requires the use of one's own knowledge and experiences.
    D. Fractions are a logical math topic.

Answer C: Choice A and C are similar. However, Choice C offers more support to the idea of English being abstract and is therefore the better answer.

22. Why did the author use the words *on the other hand* in the following sentence from the passage?

    "Math, *on the other hand,* has rules and sequences."

    A. To show that math is logical.
    B. To compare math and English as opposites.
    C. To show that fractions are like a topic in English.
    D. To demonstrate that math is better than English.

Answer B: "On the other hand" is a transitional phrase that is often used to compare to things and show opposition. Choice B is therefore, the best answer.

23. Why does the author say, "One topic in particular that often throws people a curve ball is fractions."

    A. Because fractions are useful in baseball.
    B. A baseball player must know fractions in order to throw a curve ball.
    C. A batter is often fooled by a curve ball because it is tricky.
    D. Fractions are very easy to understand just like a curve ball in baseball.

Answer C: The term, "throw for a curve ball" is a figure of speech – a metaphor. The author is comparing the pitch in baseball – the curve ball – to fractions in math and saying that both of them are tricky.

24. Does the author show any evidence of bias in this passage?

    A. Yes
    B. No

Answer A: The author shows favoritism to one side – English – and therefore shows bias.

25. What is the BEST summary for the above passage?

    A. Fractions are made up of numerators and denominators.
    B. People often say they are better at math or English, but one topic that often gives people difficulty is fractions.
    C. In order to understand fractions, English students must know the difference between proper and improper fractions.
    D. A fraction is a number that represents a part of a whole and is an important topic for all to understand.

Answer B: The reader must choose the sentence that best covers the gist of the whole passage. Choice B is the only choice that does not focus on one specific detail of the passage.

Alligators and crocodiles are not the same animal. Although both can be found in the Florida Everglades and even look alike, upon closer examination there are actually quite a few differences that _distinguish_ them from one another. A crocodile has a long narrow skull and has long jaws. Its teeth are always visible and overlap the upper jaw. An alligator has a bigger wider head and has a shorter jaw. Its teeth are only visible when its mouth is open. Despite their physical differences one overwhelming similarity between crocodiles and alligators is the fact that they are very intimidating. I for one would not want to get close enough to either of them to determine whether I can see their teeth when their mouth is closed.

26. **What does the word _distinguish_ mean in the passage?**

    A. To put out.
    B. To set apart.
    C. Are similar.
    D. To overlap.

Answer B: In the same sentence, to serve as a context clue, the word difference appears. It is the differences in the alligators and the crocodiles that set them apart from each other.

27. **How does the author support the idea that crocodiles and alligators are different?**

    A. Alligators and crocodiles are not the same animal.
    B. They both can be found in the Florida Everglades.
    C. A crocodile's teeth are visible when its mouth is closed; an alligator's are not.
    D. Alligators are more intimidating than crocodiles.

Answer C: There are two supporting details the author uses to distinguish the difference between crocodiles and alligators – their heads and their jaws. The only option offered in the choices is Choice C – the visibility of the crocodile's teeth.

28. **Who would MOST LIKELY be the most interested in reading this article?**

    A. A resident of the Florida Everglades.
    B. A zoologist that is in charge of the alligator exhibit.
    C. A copywriter for National Geographic Magazine.
    D. A student doing a report on crocodiles.

Answer D: This passage is pretty simplistic in its information. Therefore, Choices A, B, and C won't work. Choice D is the best choice.

29. What conclusion can be drawn about the author?

   A. The author finds it fascinating that alligators and crocodiles can be identified by their jaws.
   B. The author does not like reptiles – especially alligators and crocodiles.
   C. The author would only like to observe alligators or crocodiles at the zoo in a controlled environment.
   D. The author prefers crocodiles over alligators.

Answer C: When drawing conclusions, the reader must combine their own background knowledge with the information presented in the passage. From the last sentence of the passage, it is clear that the author is afraid of these reptiles and would only like to view them from a position of safety.

30. The author states that it is a fact that alligators and crocodiles are intimidating. Is this a true statement?

   A. Yes – it is a fact.
   B. No – it is an opinion.

Answer B: Regardless of whether the author says it is a fact or not, it can be argued that alligators and crocodiles are intimidating. Therefore, this is an opinion.

| Year | Unprovoked Bites [1] | | | | Provoked [2] Bites | Total Bites |
	Major [3]	Fatal	Minor [4]	Total	Total	Total
2005	6	(1)	1	7	2	9
2004	9	(2)	3	12	1	13
2003	9	(1)	1	10	2	12
2002	7	(0)	4	11	4	15
2001	11	(3)	5	16	9	25
2000	7	(0)	3	10	13	23
1999	5	(0)	5	10	6	16
1998	3	(0)	2	5	4	9
1997	3	(1)	1	4	4	8
1996	4	(0)	1	5	8	13
1995	9	(0)	4	13	9	22
1994	5	(0)	6	11	9	20
1993	8	(2)	5	13	6	19
1992	5	(0)	1	6	9	15
1991	5	(0)	5	10	10	20
1990	3	(0)	10	13	4	17
1989	4	(0)	6	10	3	13
1988	6	(1)	3	9	9	18
1987	3	(1)	6	9	4	13
1986	3	(0)	10	13	10	23
1985	4	(1)	2	6	1	7
1984	5	(1)	0	5	4	9
1983	5	(0)	1	6	3	9
1982	4	(0)	3	7	0	7
1981	5	(0)	3	8	2	10
1980	4	(0)	0	4	1	5
1979	2	(0)	0	2	0	2
1978	6	(1)	0	6	1	7
1977	13	(1)	1	14	0	14
1976	2	(0)	0	2	0	2
1975	4	(0)	0	4	1	5
1974	4	(0)	0	4	0	4
1973	3	(1)	0	3	0	3
1972	3	(0)	0	3	1	4
1971	3	(0)	0	3	0	3

Taken from: Florida Fish and Wildlife Conservation Commission Historic Alligator Bites on Humans in Florida; Last Updated 10/23/2005

31. **When did the most provoked alligator bites occur?**

   A. 2001
   B. 2000
   C. 1986
   D. 1977

Answer B: The reader has to find the correct column on the chart – the one titled, "Provoked Bites Total". 13 provoked bites occurred in 2000.

The last known case of smallpox in the United States occurred in Texas in 1949. Eight cases were reported and 1 death occurred. Smallpox has all but become extinct in the United States thanks to an English doctor named Edward Jenner. In 1796, Jenner made a stunning discovery that dairymaids who had contracted cowpox, a less serious disease than smallpox, never developed the smallpox disease even when they were exposed to it. To further solidify his discovery, Jenner infected an 8-year-old boy with cowpox and exposed the boy to smallpox 6 weeks later. Consequently, the boy did not develop any smallpox symptoms. Jenner then coined this process vaccine because the word "vaca" is a root which means "cow" in Latin.

There have been no further smallpox vaccinations given since 1972 in the United States with the exception of military personnel. Vaccines to this segment of the population ceased in 1990 and the world is still free of smallpox.

32. What MOST LIKELY resulted from this first vaccine?

    A. Other vaccinations were invented to prevent other communicable diseases.
    B. Edward Jenner won a distinguished medical research award.
    C. Many people died from cowpox and smallpox unnecessarily.
    D. Military personnel brought the disease back with them to the United States from foreign countries.

Answer A: This is a cause and effect question. Because the first vaccine was invented, other vaccinations were invented to prevent other diseases.

33. Which statement would the author most likely agree?

    A. Military personnel deserve our admiration and utmost respect.
    B. Children should not be used to test new vaccinations.
    C. Vaccinations are an important piece in keeping the United States healthy and disease free.
    D. Only people in Texas should have received the first vaccinations.

Answer C: Although Choice A is moral and admirable, Choice C is the best answer. The military personnel are only mentioned briefly at the conclusion of the passage, but the author does not offer any opinions about the US Military.

Recommended Immunization Schedule for Ages 0-6 Years

UNITED STATES • 2007

Range of recommended ages   Catch-up Immunization   Certain high-risk groups

Vaccine ▼ Age ▶	Birth	1 month	2 months	4 months	6 months	12 months	15 months	18 months	19-23 months	2-3 years	4-6 years
Hepatitis B[1]	HepB	HepB		see footnote 1		HepB				HepB Series	
Rotavirus			Rota	Rota	Rota						
Diphtheria, Tetanus, Pertussis			DTaP	DTaP	DTaP		DTaP				DTaP
Haemophilus Influenzae type b			Hib	Hib	Hib	Hib		Hib			
Pneumococcal[2]			PCV	PCV	PCV	PCV					
Inactivated Poliovirus			IPV	IPV		IPV					IPV
Influenza[3]						Influenza (Yearly)					
Measles, Mumps, Rubella						MMR					MMR
Varicella						Varicella					Varicella
Hepatitis A						HepA (2 doses)					
Meningococcal											

34. What conclusion can be drawn from the chart above?

A. Only those children in a high-risk group receive the Hepatitis A vaccine.
B. Children receive most of their vaccinations between the ages of 6 and 18 months of age.
C. Children receive most of their vaccinations at birth.
D. If a child misses a vaccination at a certain age, they are unable to receive it later.

Answer B: The key at the top of the chart shows that the light blue is the range of recommended ages for vaccinations. There is a large chunk of light blue under the 6 to 18 month range on the chart.

35. What is the main idea of the passage?

   A. Dairymaids were unable to contract the smallpox disease because their occupation made them immune.
   B. Edward Jenner was a veterinarian that stumbled upon the vaccination for smallpox.
   C. Smallpox could have been a destructive epidemic that was avoided thanks to the discovery of Dr. Edward Jenner.
   D. It is important for military personnel to get vaccinated before returning to the United States.

Answer C: The main idea has to be a sentence about the whole passage. Choice C is the only choice that covers the whole passage and not just one small detail.

36. What can be concluded from the statement, "There have been no further smallpox vaccinations given since 1972 in the United States…"

   A. Smallpox only existed in foreign countries.
   B. Smallpox was no longer a threat to the United States and people no longer needed to get vaccinated.
   C. Smallpox will make a comeback within the next few decades.
   D. It took a long time for people to accept that Jenner's vaccinations were needed and successful.

Answer B: The reader can decide using their own background knowledge and the information given in the passage that Choice B is the only feasible choice. There isn't any information in the passage to support any of the other choices as possible answers.

Recently developed within the past several years, Pilates is an exercise system that evolved from its creator Joseph Pilates as a way to strengthen both the mind and the body together. Many people have gravitated to Pilates as a way to achieve a healthy, toned appearance without looking too "bulky". In addition, Pilates increases good posture, improves flexibility and _agility_.

Pilates is very different than weight training in that it elongates the muscles while strengthening them. This is what eliminates the "bulky" look achieved by lifting weights. Building the core is a focus in Pilates. The core refers to the center of the body or the abdomen. People are drawn to Pilates because it helps to tone and flatten the hard to tame abdominal area.

Safety is another benefit that Pilates boasts. If the muscles of the body are trained in a fluid, smooth motion and technique, the muscles will work more efficiently and posture will be improved and injuries will be prevented.

37. Why might people be interested in Pilates?

    A. They want to get bulkier looking muscles.
    B. They want to increase their cardiovascular endurance.
    C. They want to tone their muscles and improve their posture.
    D. They want to have Joseph Pilates personally train them.

Answer C: Choice A is the opposite of what Pilates strives to accomplish and Choice B is incorrect because Pilates is not a cardiovascular building exercise. Although Joseph Pilates is the founder of Pilates, he will not personally train them. Therefore, Choice C is the best choice.

38. When the author says that, "Pilates increases good posture, improves flexibility and agility," that is a(n)

    A. Fact
    B. Opinion

Answer A: This is a fact and is the foundation in which Pilates was founded.

39. From the passage, it can be assumed that

    A. Only celebrities and those with a lot of money can do Pilates training.
    B. Pilates training would be a beneficial mode of exercise for all ages.
    C. Dancers will greatly benefit from doing Pilates daily.
    D. Joseph Pilates only developed this form of exercise because he did not enjoy running.

Answer B: Choices B and C are the best two answers, and although dancers will benefit from doing Pilates, they are not the only specific group. Therefore, Choice B is the best because it is true and applies to a much broader base of people.

40. Which is the best synonym for the word <u>agility</u>?

    A. relationships
    B. power
    C. endurance
    D. self-confidence

Answer C: Choices B and C would be acceptable, but the best answer, according to the context clues available in the passage that tell us that Pilates is a strength building exercise program – Choice C is the best answer.

41. What is another way the information in the passage could be delivered?

    A. A poster.
    B. An infomercial.
    C. A Venn Diagram
    D. A before and after diagram

Answer B: An infomercial is a form of media that is a step beyond the commercial. It offers a lot more information while trying to sell something. People might be persuaded in an infomercial to try Pilates.

42. What two components are Pilates aimed at improving?

    A. The mind and the body together.
    B. The muscles and the core.
    C. The abdominal area and the mind.
    D. The legs and the core.

Answer A: Although Pilates aims at improving all of the components listed, it strictly focuses on improving the mind to control the body. This is a detail that the reader must find in the passage.

Writing Post Test Rationales

1 Nursing is a great career for women who have or want to have young children someday. **2** They can work very flexible schedules either part time or full time. **3** healthcare is an ever expanding feild so jobs are predicted to be plentiful in many years to come. **4** There are many different areas where people can match their interests to a particular nursing specialty. **5** For example, if one is interested in children, the elderly, or feet even, there is a place for everyone. **6** Even though there are a lot of positive reasons for women to choose nursing as a career, the negatives must also be considered before embarking on a lifelong career choice.

1. **What would be the best way to combine sentences 1 and 2 to make a complete topic sentence?**

    A. Nursing is a great career for women who have, or want to have children someday, because the schedules are flexible and offer a lot of full and part time opportunities.
    B. Nursing is a great career for women who have, or want to have children on the other hand it offers flexible full and part time schedules.
    C. Nursing is a great career for women who currently have, or want to have, a family due to the full and part time flexible scheduling.
    D. Nursing is a great career for women who currently have, or want to have, a family furthermore because of the full time and part time scheduling.

Answer A: Although the topic sentence is fine as is, in order to combine sentence 1 and 2 a transition word is needed. The best transition word to use in this instance is "because". Choice C will not work because it sounds like women might want to have a family because of the flexible scheduling it offers.

2. **Which of these ideas does not help to develop the main idea of the passage?**

    A. Healthcare is an ever expanding field.
    B. People can match their interests to a particular field in nursing.
    C. Even people interested in feet can become a nurse.
    D. There are negative aspects to any job.

Answer D: Choices A, B, and C all support the main idea of why nursing is a great career for women. Choice D gets off on a tangent from the main idea.

3. **Which part of the passage should be corrected to use the correct relative pronoun?**

   A. Part 1: Change "whom" to "who"
   B. Part 3: Change "so" to "that"
   C. Part 4: Change "where" to "which"
   D. Part 6: Change "on" to "in"

Answer A: The relative pronoun "whom" is only used to refer to a singular noun. For example, "Whom did you take to the movies?" In this passage, "whom" follows women so it needs to be "who".

4. **Which verb needs to be changed to make the sentence correct?**

   A. Part 1: occurring
   B. Part 2: rode
   C. Part 3: aware
   D. Part 4: riding

Answer B: The word "works" needs to be "work" even though the word "schedules" is plural.

5. **Which word is misspelled?**

   A. Part 1: someday
   B. Part 2: flexible
   C. Part 3: feild
   D. Part 6: though

Answer C: The correct spelling is "field". Remember the saying, "I before e except after c, except for in words like neighbor and weigh".

6. **How should sentence 5 be rewritten?**

   A. For example, if one is interested in children – the elderly – or feet – even there is a place for everyone.
   B. For example if one is interested in children, the elderly feet, or even there is a place for everyone.
   C. For example, if one is interested in children, the elderly, or feet even, there is a place for everyone.
   D. For example: if one is interested in children – the elderly; or feet even, there is a place for everyone.

Answer C: The original sentence in the passage was missing commas in a series. The sentence is listing things that someone might be interested in therefore commas are required to separate these ideas.

7. **What needs to be capitalized in the passage?**

   A. Part 1: Women
   B. Part 3: Healthcare
   C. Part 5: Elderly
   D. Part 6: Nursing

Answer B: Healthcare is the first word of the sentence and requires a capital letter. There aren't any proper nouns in this passage, so there aren't any other words (besides first words of sentences) that must be capitalized.

1 The school staff at Lincoln Middle School was not prepared for the increase in the number of students whom would be entering the 6th grade in the upcoming school year. **2** Several changes needed to be made in order to accommodate the largely intended increase in the student body. **3** First another classroom needed to be found. **4** This would be a daunting task but there were several possibilities to consider. **5** Moving the computer lab was one option. **6** More computers could be added to the library and the other four labs that were spred around the building. **7** Lincoln middle would be short a computer lab, but would have gained another classroom. **8** Next, a new staff member would have to be hired to work inside the new classroom. **9** This too would not be a problem because there was an over abundance of applicants that had applied for teaching positions that year. **10** The biggest problem would be the amount of teaching resources available. **11** More textbooks and workbooks would need to be ordered. **12** It was questionable if the teachers resources would all arrive in time for the new school year to begin.

8. **If a new paragraph was to be started at line 3, what would be the best transitional phrase to use?**

    A. Last but not least,
    B. In the meantime,
    C. First and foremost,
    D. The first thing at hand,

Answer C: The way the passage reads now, first is a great transition word to use. However, if another paragraph was to be started, then more information would need to be inserted. Therefore, Choice C is the best answer that most relates to the single word "first".

9. **Which part of the passage should be revised to correct an error in the use of prepositions?**

    A. Part 1: Change "at" to "in"
    B. Part 2: Change "in" to "of"
    C. Part 8: Change "inside" to "in"
    D. Part 12: Change "in" to "on"

Answer C: Although both of these options, "inside" and "in" would work, the better choice is, "in the new classroom".

10. Which word is misspelled?

    A. Part 1: increase
    B. Part 5: four
    C. Part 5: spred
    D. Part 10: biggest

Answer C: The correct spelling of the word is "spread". Even though "ea" together normally makes the long e sound, in words like spread, bread, tread etc. the combination makes the short e sound.

11. Which word needs a change in capitalization?

    A. Part 1: Lincoln
    B. Part 1: grade
    C. Part 7: middle
    D. Part 12: school year

Answer C: Choice A is a proper noun and should have a capital letter. Choices B and D are common nouns and do not require a capital. The word "middle" requires a capital because it goes with the proper noun Lincoln as a name of the school.

12. Which part of the passage requires a comma?

    A. Part 1: The school staff at Lincoln Middle School, was not prepared for the increase in the number of students whom would be entering the 6th grade in the upcoming school year.
    B. Part 3: First, another classroom needed to be found.
    C. Part 6: More computers could be added to the library, and the other four labs that were spread around the building.
    D. Part 9: This too, would not be a problem because there was an over abundance of applicants that had applied for teaching positions that year.

Answer B: The transition word for sequencing, "first", needs a comma after it. All transition words need to be followed by a comma when they are used as introductory words in a sentence.

13. **Which part of the passage requires an apostrophe?**

    A. Part 1: students
    B. Part 4: possibilities
    C. Part 6: computers
    D. Part 12: teachers

Answer D: Choices A, B, and C are all just plural nouns that do not show any possessions and therefore do not require an apostrophe. Choice D refers to the teacher's resources so it requires an apostrophe.

1 Their are many things living objects need in order to survive. **2** All living things need food, water, and air. **3** Plants get their food from the rich nutrients in soil, water from rain and they pull air in through their leaves. **4** Animals get food by hunting pray, they too get water from rain, but find sources where it has collected, and they get their air from the oxygen that plants and trees emit. **5** Humans are like animals. **6** We need food water, and air to survive. **7** We have an overabundance of food and water supplies and feel that we cannot live without food. **8** However, we can live without food for several weeks if necessary. **9** We can survive without water for only a few days. **10** However we can only live without air for as little as 3 to 6 minutes. **11** Air is essential for humans hearts and brains to function properly.

14. **If another paragraph were to be added, what would be the best topic sentence?**

    A. Humans think that food and water are the most important things needed for their survival.
    B. When humans breathe air into their lungs it serves several different purposes.
    C. Humans and animals are alike because both require oxygen for their survival.
    D. When humans consume food, it goes through several processes in order to be turned into fuel for the human body.

Answer B: The first paragraph concluded talking about how air is essential for the heart and brain to function properly. Therefore, the next paragraph must tie in this idea to its main idea. The main idea of the second paragraph will clearly be to discuss what happens to the oxygen after it enters the body and how it benefits humans.

15. **Which sentence could be deleted from the passage because of redundancy?**

    A. Sentence 7
    B. Sentence 8
    C. Sentence 9
    D. Sentence 10

Answer A: Sentence 7 continues to talk about food. But if it were deleted, sentence 8 further details the idea that humans require food. It explains further that we can live without food for several weeks if necessary.

16. Which sentence should have a period instead of a comma?

    A. Sentence 2
    B. Sentence 4
    C. Sentence 6
    D. Sentence 7

Answer B: Sentence 4 is a run on sentence. The sentence should read, "Animals get food by hunting prey. They too get water from rain, but find sources where it has collected, and they get their air from the oxygen that plants and trees emit."

17. What is the correct way to revise sentence 6?

    A. We, need food, water, and air to survive.
    B. We need food, water and air to survive.
    C. We need food water and air to survive.
    D. We need food, water, and air to survive.

Answer D: Commas are required in a series of items that are listed. Commas are also required before the word "and" when commas appear in a series. Therefore, Choice D is the best answer.

18. How should sentence 7 be revised to be clearer?

    A. In the United States, there is an overabundance of food and water.
    B. Supplies of food and water are in overabundance within the United States for humans.
    C. Food and water supplies in abundance are available in a plentiful manner in the United States.
    D. An overabundance of food and water and air is available for citizens of the United States.

Answer A: This is the most straight forward, way to rephrase what is written in the passage. The other choices are all very wordy and often don't make sense.

19. Which sentence contains the wrong form of their/there/they're?

    A. Sentence 1
    B. Sentence 3
    C. Sentence 4
    D. Sentence 11

Answer A: There is used to mark a place; their shows possession. "They're" is a contraction for the two words they are. Sentence 1 needs to have the word "there" because the contraction won't work in this instance.

20. Which sentence has a misspelled word in it?

    A. Sentence 4
    B. Sentence 5
    C. Sentence 6
    D. Sentence 7

Answer A: Sentence 4 has the word "pray" misspelled. The correct spelling is "prey". Pray is a religious saying; prey is something that is hunted.

21. Which sentence is missing a comma?

    A. Sentence 1
    B. Sentence 3
    C. Sentence 5
    D. Sentence 10

Answer D: Introductory, or transition words, need a comma after them. The word "however" is an introductory word that requires a transition after it.

22. Which sentence needs an apostrophe added?

    A. Sentence 3
    B. Sentence 4
    C. Sentence 5
    D. Sentence 11

Answer D: An apostrophe is required in words to show possession. In sentence 11, the hearts and brains belong to the humans. Therefore, the word humans requires an apostrophe.

1 Earthquakes are sometimes something to fear. **2** With the invention of the seismograph however, they have become more predictable. **3** Scientists has predicted the potential for earthquakes with a reasonable degree of accuracy. **4** Sometimes even scientists have predicted an earthquake but it has never occurred. **5** Some believe that this is a good mistake. **6** It is better to have predicted an Earthquake incorrectly than not predict it at all.

23. **What is the topic sentence of the passage?**

   A. Sentence 1
   B. Sentence 2
   C. Sentence 3
   D. Sentence 4

Answer B: Normally a topic sentence is the first sentence of the paragraph. But a topic sentence states what the main idea of the passage or paragraph is going to be. In this case, the paragraph is talking about the seismograph machine and how predicting earthquakes is now improved.

24. **Which sentence shows some redundancy?**

   A. Sentence 3
   B. Sentence 4
   C. Sentence 9
   D. Sentence 11

Answer B: Sentence 4 is awkward because of redundancy. The sentence should simply read, "Sometimes scientists have predicted…" deleting the "even" from the sentence.

25. **If another paragraph were to be added to this passage, what is the best topic sentence?**

   A. One earthquake that scientists were able to predict by using a seismograph was X.
   B. The definition of an earthquake is…
   C. The biggest earthquake to hit the United States was…
   D. Earthquakes have been recorded the most in…

Answer A: The last sentence of the first paragraph says that it is better to have predicted an earthquake incorrectly than not predict it at all. Therefore, the next sentence of the next paragraph must tie into this idea to connect the two paragraphs. Choice A is the best answer that will accomplish this task.

26. **Which sentence has a verb in its incorrect form?**

   A. Sentence 1
   B. Sentence 3
   C. Sentence 4
   D. Sentence 6

Answer B: The word "has" needs to be changed to "have" so the sentence reads, "Scientists have predicted the potential for earthquakes with a reasonable degree of accuracy".

27. **Which sentence has misplaced or dangling modifiers?**

   A. Sentence 1
   B. Sentence 2
   C. Sentence 3
   D. Sentence 4

Answer B: The word they can mean either the earthquakes or the seismograph. The sentence needs to read something like this, "With the invention of the seismograph however, earthquakes have become more predicatable."

28. **Which sentence contains an error in capitalization?**

   A. Sentence 4
   B. Sentence 5
   C. Sentence 6
   D. Sentence 7

Answer C: The word "Earthquake" should not be capitalized. If a particular name of an earthquake were given, then it would need to be capitalized because it would be a proper noun. As it reads now, earthquake is a common noun and does not require a capital letter.

29. **Which sentence is missing a comma?**

   A. Sentence 3
   B. Sentence 4
   C. Sentence 9
   D. Sentence 12

Answer B: There should be a comma after sometimes so that the reader will pause after reading the introductory word, "sometimes". This is evident because the sentence would still make sense if the word "sometimes" was taken out altogether.

30. **Which topic would be the best focus for the introduction to come before the first sentence of this passage?**

    A. Inventions
    B. Famous scientists
    C. Things we are scared of
    D. Things that shake

Answer C: An introductory paragraph should start off broad and become narrowed. To talk about fear and then narrow the paragraph to earthquakes would grab the reader's attention from the very beginning.

1 Certain plants and animals have been able to adapt well to the extreme conditions of the desert. **2** Since there is very little water available in the desert plants and animals have had to evolve and change. **3** Some things that are unique to plants in the desert are their thick leaves. **4** The thick leaves are vats used for storing water. **5** One such plant that has adapted very successfully is the cactus. **6** But the cactus doesn't stop there! **7** It even protects its supply of water with its long pointy spines. **8** These spines keep predators from tapping into the cacti's thick, succulent leaves. **9** Water is stored in the leaves of the cactus.

31. **What is the thesis statement for this essay?**

      A. Sentence 1
      B. Sentence 2
      C. Sentence 3
      D. Sentence 4

Answer A: The thesis statement states the main idea of an essay. The main idea of this essay is how plants and animals have adapted to the extreme dry conditions of the desert.

32. **Which sentence does not contribute to the development of the main idea of the passage?**

      A. Sentence 5
      B. Sentence 6
      C. Sentence 7
      D. Sentence 1

Answer A: Although it is fine to have this type of interest sentence in an essay or paragraph, it is the one sentence that does not contribute to the development of the main idea of the passage.

33. **Which sentence should come first in the next paragraph if the essay were to be continued?**

      A. Not even a small hummingbird would try to penetrate the spines of a cactus.
      B. Many people have be pricked by the spines of a cactus.
      C. One animal that has adapted well to the extreme conditions of the desert is the Gila Monster.
      D. People are not able to live in the desert for long periods of time because of the lack of moisture.

Answer C: The thesis statement, the first sentence of the passage, states that both plants and animals have been able to adapt well to the extreme conditions of the desert. Therefore, it logically follows that the next part of the essay would have to be about the animals that have adapted to the extreme conditions of the desert.

34. **Which sentence could be deleted from the passage because it is repetitive?**

    A. Sentence 6
    B. Sentence 7
    C. Sentence 8
    D. Sentence 9

Answer C: Sentence 8 is not necessary to the development of the passage and can be deleted because the same thing is stated in sentence 4 and is further explained in sentence 6. Therefore, sentence 8 is unnecessary.

35. **What would be the best way to combine sentences 1 and 2 to create a new topic sentence?**

    A. Due to the extremely dry conditions in the desert, the plants and animals that survive there have had to adapt.
    B. The plants and animals that call the desert their home are able to do so because they have adapted to the extremely dry conditions there.
    C. No water means that plants and animals have had to adapt.
    D. The desert causes the things that live there to adapt to its conditions.

Answer B: Choices C and D do not contain enough detail. Choices A and B are both good choices, but Choice B is more fluent and better written.

The following sentences contain two errors each (e.g., in construction, grammar, usage, spelling, capitalization, punctuation). Rewrite the text so that the errors are addressed and the original meaning is maintained.

36. **Mozart used an instrument called the harpsichord and the piano to create a lot of beautiful concertos which are still enjoy today.**

    Answer: The word instrument does not agree with harsichord *and* piano. Therefore, the word must be "instruments". The word "enjoy" needs to be "enjoyed". The new sentence should read:

    Mozart used the instruments, the harpsichord and the piano, to create a lot of beautiful concertos which are still enjoyed today.

37. **A teacher must be savvy when grading research and term papers and have the ability to recognize plagiarizing student work.**

    Answer: There should be a comma after the word "papers" and before "and". "Plagiarizing" needs to be changed to "plagiarism" and "in" needs to be added. The new sentence should read:

    A teacher must be savvy when grading research and term papers, and have the ability to recognize plagiarism in student work.

38. **After watching the two commercials back to back that was trying to sell the same product I came to the conclusion that the first commercial was more interesting than the second one.**

    Answer: The verb was needs to be were, and a comma is needed after the word product. The new sentence should read:

    After watching the two commercials back to back that were trying to sell the same product, I came to the conclusion that the first commercial was more interesting than the second one.

39. **Upon checking the applicants references the company found that the candidate was not as reliable as was initially believed to be.**

> **Answer:** The references belong to the applicant so an apostrophe is needed to show possession. A comma is needed after references because it is a dependent clause. The new sentence should read:

> *Upon checking the applicant's references, the company found that the candidate was not as reliable as was initially believed to be.*

40. **The woman gathered together at the house of there friend Nancy to discuss the current political agenda.**

> **Answer:** The plural form of woman is "women". The word "there" is the wrong word and needs to be "their". The new sentence should read:

> *The women gathered together at the house of their friend Nancy to discuss the current political agenda.*

41. **The pie had a flaky crusts that made it deliciously and irresistible.**

> **Answer:** Crusts needs to be singular. Deliciously is the wrong form of the word. The new sentence should read:

> *The pie had a flaky crust that made it delicious and irresistible.*

42. **Less U.S. citizens are visiting European countries because of the dwindles in the current exchange rate.**

> **Answer:** The correct word to use is "fewer" not "less". The word "dwindles" should be singular. The new sentence should read:

> *Fewer U.S. citizens are visiting European countries because of the dwindle in the current exchange rate.*

Essay #1: **Use the passage below to prepare a summary of 100-150 words.**

Curriculums within schools are the depth and breadth of the education the students will receive. They are living breathing documents which provide the foundation for the entire educational process in this country. Curriculums are necessary evils to many developers; complex structures which grow, change, and never seem to be quite finished. In the ideal, the curriculum is what is taught to the students, the content. It is through this content that learners societal and subject matter needs are all addressed.

Historically, curriculums have not always been as influential as designers would like them for the students they serve. In recent times, more attention has been paid to the manner in which curriculum effects what is actually being taught in classrooms. Federal and State mandates have imposed this increase in attention. Governmental influence into education has steadily increased reaching its ebb in 2001 with the passage of the No Child Left Behind (NCLB) legislation.

While the legislation itself does not require a federally aligned or mandated curriculum, it does hold schools accountable for making progress. This accountability piece is within itself a demand for curriculum accountability. States have imposed a variety of mandates in order to meet these requirements some in the form of required assessments and standards which

provide schools with a broad general focus upon which to build their curriculums.

Reaching its pinnacle for discussion in the 1990s, the standards-based reform movement provides schools with a basis upon which to build their own individual curriculums. As adopted this movement provides individual school entities the basic understanding of areas which need to be covered by the curriculum at specific target grade levels. These same areas are then assessed utilizing state level assessments, thus tracking progress and providing accountability in order to meet the requirements of the NCLB Act.

At this point, it becomes the responsibility of the school entity to transfer this broad standard level information into a meaningful curriculum which is then delivered to its students. The school system typically takes this broad information provided for key benchmark grade levels and breaks it into meaningful, developmentally appropriate chunks to cover all grade levels and subjects. Systems must also consider skills beyond those being assessed which are important aspects in order to provide a broader more appropriate curriculum, rather than a narrow, only what is assessed one.

Standards-based education has taken the understanding of schools and systems to a higher level in regards to the content. However, with the passage of NCLB many curriculums have unfortunately narrowed to a scope which is only inclusive of the areas being assessed at targeted grade levels. It will be throughout the next few years that systems will have to combine the ideas of standards-based educational reform with best practices in curriculum development to reach a compromise which meets the needs of all students within its system. The combination of both approaches will help to move students to higher levels of academic success, which can only serve to move the entire society to higher levels as well.

Curriculums are tools school systems use to ensure their students are learning the appropriate types and amounts of information to be successful in society. Curriculums change regularly as societal needs change. Standards-based reforms began in the 1990s and provided systems with a list of the basic standards each state felt were important for students at specific grade levels to meet. As standards-based reform has become an important part of education, curriculums have shifted to focus only on specific standards rather than the broad scope of the past. In this way, students are being short changed. It is the hope that as standards-based reforms are better understood, curriculums can adapt and once again broaden in their scope.

Standards-based reforms have led to problems with curriculums. School systems have to figure out ways to improve their own curriculums to be able to meet the standards set forth by the state. Because so many curriculums are not well done or don't change fast enough, schools are not able to meet the standards the state sets for them. Other times systems don't think the standards are correct or important so they don't try to achieve them. It is the students who suffer. Curriculums and standards have to work together for students to be successful.

Essay #2: Read the passages that follow about drug testing in schools. Then follow the instructions for writing your composition.

Drug Testing in Schools Is Necessary to Eliminate the amount of Drug Addicts in Society

School systems have a responsibility to educate and protect their students. By employing the use of drug tests, schools can provide additional education opportunities to ensure students do not become addicts. Additionally, it sends the message to all members that drugs are wrong.

Drug Testing in Schools is Wrong

Schools are places for learning, not police action. Students in schools have the right to privacy and should not be considered guilty until proven innocent when the same standard is not applied to other portions of society. While drug use is a problem, it is not the responsibility of the school system to risk the dignity of all students based on a fear of what a few students may be engaged in during their off school time.

Your purpose is to write a composition that will be read by a classroom instructor, in which you will take a position on the issues described in the passages about drug testing in schools. Be sure to use logical arguments to defend your position and include appropriate examples.

Sample Well-Done Response:

School systems are places for providing an education in a safe environment. While safety is a standard which cannot be diminished, it is not the responsibility of schools to become a police state. When schools implement mandatory drug testing for all students, school systems indeed become police states. Mandatory drug testing should not occur in public school systems as it violates the individual rights of its students, does nothing to prevent drug abuse which cannot be achieved through other means, and invades the privacy of all students.

As schools implement mandatory drug testing, they are implying that students are indeed committing a crime. The thinking has shifted from one where students are innocent until they can be proven guilty to one where students are guilty; it is just a matter of finding which ones. This notion is not one supported by the criminal justice system and therefore should not be implemented.

Additionally, the use of mandatory drug testing has in no way been proven to prevent further drug abuse. In fact, there are many other methods of prevention which have been shown to be more effective at preventing later drug abuse such as: parental education, relief of poverty, and engagement in extra-curricular activities.

Finally, the use of mandatory drug testing in schools violates the basic rights of students to their own privacy. Students could be mistakenly identified as using drugs leading to issues of self-esteem. Of utmost importance is the protection of the dignity of the students. Loss of self-esteem and dignity will impede the ability of the students to engage in the academic tasks they are in school to learn.

In the end, schools are places to foster critical and reflective thinking about many issues. Mandatory drug testing only serves to impede this ability as students become resentful. Therefore, it should not be implemented within schools.

Sample Poor Response:

Schools should not implement mandatory drug testing because it is wrong. Schools are not places where students should have to take a drug test. They are there to learn. The budgets of schools are already stretched so thin, that spending the money on drug testing will result in poorer academic skills. Also, students are going to take drugs regardless of whether or not they are going to be tested. In fact, students will spend the time they should be learning academics, learning to beat the test. This isn't what schools should be spending their time doing.